✳ *Makes 12 muffins*

Hearty Banana Carrot Muffins

2 ripe, medium DOLE® Bananas
1 package (14 ounces) oat bran muffin mix
3/4 teaspoon ground ginger
1 medium DOLE® Carrot, shredded (1/2 cup)
1/3 cup light molasses
1/3 cup DOLE® Seedless or Golden Raisins
1/4 cup chopped almonds

✳ Mash bananas with fork (1 cup).

✳ Combine muffin mix and ginger in large bowl. Add carrot, molasses, raisins and bananas. Stir just until moistened.

✳ Spoon batter into paper-lined muffin cups. Sprinkle tops with almonds.

✳ Bake at 425°F 12 to 14 minutes until browned.

Prep Time: 20 minutes ✳ **Bake Time:** 14 minutes

> Oats of Wisdom: Light and dark molasses are interchangeable in recipes. Dark molasses has a slightly more robust flavor.

Oat and Whole Wheat Scones

1 cup uncooked old-fashioned oats
1 cup whole wheat flour
$1/2$ cup all-purpose flour
$1/4$ cup sugar
1 tablespoon baking powder
$1/4$ teaspoon salt
$1/2$ cup (1 stick) unsalted butter, cut into small pieces
$1/2$ cup whipping cream
1 egg
$3/4$ cup dried cherries

1. Preheat oven to 425°F. Line baking sheet with parchment paper; set aside.

2. Combine oats, flours, sugar, baking powder and salt in large bowl. Cut in butter with pastry blender or fork until mixture resembles coarse crumbs.

3. Beat cream and egg in small bowl; stir into flour mixture until dough comes together. Stir in cherries.

4. Turn dough out onto lightly floured surface. Shape dough into 8-inch round, about $3/4$ inch thick. Cut into 8 wedges. Place 1 inch apart on prepared baking sheet. Bake 18 minutes or until golden brown.

❊ *Makes 1 braided wreath or 2 loaves*

Wild Rice Three Grain Bread

1 package active dry yeast
$^{1}/_{3}$ cup warm water (105° to 115°F)
2 cups milk, scalded and cooled to 105° to 115°F
$^{1}/_{2}$ cup honey
2 tablespoons butter, melted
2 teaspoons salt
4 to $4^{1}/_{2}$ cups bread flour or unbleached all-purpose flour
2 cups whole wheat flour
$^{1}/_{2}$ cup rye flour
$^{1}/_{2}$ cup uncooked rolled oats
1 cup cooked wild rice
1 egg, beaten with 1 tablespoon water
$^{1}/_{2}$ cup hulled sunflower seeds

In large bowl, dissolve yeast in water. Add milk, honey, butter and salt. Stir in 2 cups bread flour, whole wheat flour, rye flour and oats to make a soft dough. Add wild rice; cover and let rest 15 minutes. Stir in enough additional bread flour to make a stiff dough. Turn dough out onto board and knead 10 minutes. Add more flour as necessary to keep dough from sticking. Turn dough into lightly greased bowl; turn dough over to coat. Cover and let rise until doubled, about 2 hours. Punch down dough. Knead briefly on lightly oiled board. To shape dough, divide into 3 portions; roll into long strands. Braid strands and place on greased baking sheet in wreath shape, or divide in half and place each half in greased $9^{1}/_{2} \times 5^{1}/_{2}$-inch loaf pans. Let rise until doubled, about 45 minutes. Brush tops of loaves with egg mixture; slash loaves if desired. Sprinkle with sunflower seeds. Bake at 375°F 45 minutes or until loaves sound hollow when tapped.

Favorite recipe from **Minnesota Cultivated Wild Rice Council**

✖ *Makes 1 (1½-pound) loaf*

Good Morning Bread

¼ cup water
1 cup mashed ripe bananas (about 3 medium)
3 tablespoons vegetable oil
1 teaspoon salt
2¼ cups bread flour
¾ cup whole wheat flour
¾ cup chopped pitted dates
½ cup uncooked old-fashioned oats
¼ cup nonfat dry milk powder
1 teaspoon grated orange peel (optional)
1 teaspoon ground cinnamon
2 teaspoons active dry yeast

BREAD MACHINE DIRECTIONS

1. Measuring carefully, place all ingredients in bread machine pan in order specified by owner's manual.

2. Program basic cycle and desired crust setting; press start. Immediately remove baked bread from pan; cool on wire rack.

Note: This recipe produces a moist, slightly dense loaf that has a lower volume than other loaves. The banana flavor is more prominent when the bread is toasted.

Creative Cookie Classics

✻ *Makes about 2 dozen cookies*

Pumpkin Oatmeal Cookies

    1 cup all-purpose flour
    1 teaspoon ground cinnamon
    1/2 teaspoon salt
    1/2 teaspoon ground nutmeg
    1/4 teaspoon baking soda
  1 1/2 cups packed light brown sugar
    1/2 cup (1 stick) butter, softened
    1 egg
    1 teaspoon vanilla
    1/2 cup solid-pack pumpkin
    2 cups uncooked old-fashioned oats
    1 cup dried cranberries (optional)

1. Preheat oven to 350°F. Line cookie sheets with parchment paper.

2. Sift flour, cinnamon, salt, nutmeg and baking soda into medium bowl. Beat brown sugar and butter in large bowl with electric mixer at medium speed about 5 minutes or until light and fluffy.

3. Beat in egg and vanilla. Add pumpkin; beat at low speed until blended. Beat in flour mixture just until blended. Add oats; mix well. Stir in cranberries, if desired. Drop dough by rounded tablespoonfuls 2 inches apart onto prepared cookie sheets.

4. Bake 12 minutes or until golden brown. Cool 1 minute on cookie sheets. Remove to wire racks; cool completely.

�֍ ✻ ✻ ✻

❋ *Makes about 4 dozen cookies*

Chocolate Oatmeal Chippers

1¼ cups all-purpose flour
½ cup NESTLÉ® TOLL HOUSE® Baking Cocoa
1 teaspoon baking soda
¼ teaspoon salt
1 cup (2 sticks) butter or margarine, softened
1 cup packed brown sugar
½ cup granulated sugar
1 teaspoon vanilla extract
2 eggs
1¾ cups (11½-ounce package) NESTLÉ® TOLL HOUSE® Milk
    Chocolate Morsels
1¾ cups quick or old-fashioned oats
1 cup chopped nuts (optional)

PREHEAT oven to 375°F.

COMBINE flour, cocoa, baking soda and salt in medium bowl. Beat butter, brown sugar, granulated sugar and vanilla in large mixer bowl until creamy. Beat in eggs. Gradually beat in flour mixture. Stir in morsels, oats and nuts. Drop dough by rounded tablespoon onto ungreased baking sheets.

BAKE for 9 to 12 minutes or until edges are set but centers are still soft. Cool on baking sheets for 2 minutes; remove to wire racks to cool completely.

Bar Cookie Variation: PREHEAT oven to 350°F. Grease 15×10-inch jelly-roll pan. Prepare dough as above. Spread into prepared pan. Bake for 25 to 30 minutes. Cool in pan on wire rack. Makes about 4 dozen bars.

✳ *Makes about 4 dozen cookies*

Gingery Oat and Molasses Cookies

    1 cup all-purpose flour
    3/4 cup whole wheat flour
    1/2 cup uncooked old-fashioned oats
    1 1/2 teaspoons baking powder
    1 1/2 teaspoons ground ginger
    1 teaspoon baking soda
    1/2 teaspoon ground cinnamon
    1/4 teaspoon salt
    3/4 cup sugar
    1/2 cup (1 stick) unsalted butter, softened
    1/4 cup molasses
    1 egg
    1/4 teaspoon vanilla
    1 cup chopped crystallized ginger
    1/2 cup chopped walnuts

1. Grease cookie sheets; set aside. Combine flours, oats, baking powder, ground ginger, baking soda, cinnamon and salt in large bowl; set aside.

2. Beat sugar and butter in large bowl with electric mixer at high speed until light and fluffy. Beat in molasses, egg and vanilla. Gradually mix in flour mixture. Stir in crystallized ginger and walnuts. Shape into 2 logs about 10 inches long. Wrap in plastic wrap; chill 1 to 3 hours.

3. Preheat oven to 350°F. Cut 1/3-inch slices with sharp knife. Arrange 1 1/2 inches apart on prepared cookie sheets. Bake 12 to 14 minutes or until cookies are firm and browned at edges. Cool 5 minutes on cookie sheets. Remove to wire rack; cool completely.

❋ *Makes about 4 dozen biscotti*

Oat, Chocolate and Hazelnut Biscotti

1¹/₂ cups whole wheat flour
1 cup all-purpose flour
1 cup uncooked old-fashioned oats
2 teaspoons baking powder
¹/₂ teaspoon salt
¹/₂ teaspoon ground cinnamon
1¹/₂ cups sugar
¹/₂ cup (1 stick) unsalted butter, at room temperature
3 eggs
1 teaspoon vanilla
2 cups toasted whole hazelnuts
³/₄ cup semisweet chocolate chunks

1. Preheat oven to 325°F. Line cookie sheet with parchment paper.

2. Combine flours, oats, baking powder, salt and cinnamon in large bowl. Beat sugar and butter in large bowl with electric mixer at high speed until light and fluffy. Beat in eggs and vanilla. Gradually mix in flour mixture. Stir in hazelnuts and chocolate chunks.

3. Divide dough in half. Shape into logs 10 to 12 inches long; flatten slightly to 3-inch width. Place on cookie sheet. Bake 30 minutes. Cool completely on baking sheet.

4. *Reduce oven temperature to 300°F.* Transfer logs to cutting board. Cut diagonal slices about ¹/₂ inch thick using serrated knife. Arrange slices on cookie sheet. Bake 10 to 15 minutes or until golden. Turn slices over and bake 5 to 10 minutes or until golden. Remove to wire rack; cool completely.

Oats of Wisdom: To toast hazelnuts, preheat oven to 325°F. Spread hazelnuts on baking sheet. Toast 5 to 7 minutes; remove from oven. Place nuts in a kitchen towel and rub to remove skins.

Cookie Dough Bears

1 package (about 18 ounces) refrigerated sugar cookie dough
1 cup uncooked quick oats
  Mini semisweet chocolate chips

1. Combine cookie dough and oats in medium bowl; mix well. Cover and freeze 15 minutes.

2. Meanwhile, preheat oven to 350°F. Lightly spray cookie sheets with nonstick cooking spray. For each bear, shape 1 (1-inch) ball for body and 1 (³/₄-inch) ball for head. Place body and head together on cookie sheet; flatten slightly. Form 7 small balls for arms, legs, ears and nose; arrange on bear body and head. Place 2 chocolate chips on each head for eyes. Place 1 chocolate chip on each body for belly button.

3. Bake 12 to 14 minutes or until edges are lightly browned. Cool bears 2 minutes on cookie sheets. Remove to wire racks; cool completely.

Fudgy Oatmeal Butterscotch Cookies

1 package (18.25 ounces) devil's food cake mix
1¹/₂ cups quick-cooking or old-fashioned oats, uncooked
³/₄ cup (1¹/₂ sticks) butter, melted
2 large eggs
1 tablespoon vegetable oil
1 teaspoon vanilla extract
1¹/₄ cups "M&M's"® Chocolate Mini Baking Bits
1 cup butterscotch chips

Preheat oven to 350°F. In large bowl, combine cake mix, oats, butter, eggs, oil and vanilla until well blended. Stir in "M&M's"® Chocolate Mini Baking Bits and butterscotch chips. Drop by heaping tablespoonfuls about 2 inches apart onto ungreased cookie sheets. Bake 10 to 12 minutes. Cool 1 minute on cookie sheets. Cool completely on wire racks. Store in tightly covered container.

Double Chocolate Coconut Oatmeal Cookies

    1 cup shortening
1³/₄ cups packed light brown sugar
    3 eggs
    2 teaspoons vanilla extract
1¹/₃ cups all-purpose flour
 ¹/₂ cup HERSHEY'S Cocoa
    2 teaspoons baking soda
 ¹/₄ teaspoon salt
 ¹/₂ cup water
    3 cups uncooked old-fashioned oats or quick-cooking oats
    2 cups (12-ounce package) HERSHEY'S SPECIAL DARK Chocolate
        Chips or HERSHEY'S Semi-Sweet Chocolate Chips, divided
    2 cups MOUNDS® Sweetened Coconut Flakes, divided
    1 cup coarsely chopped nuts

1. Beat shortening, brown sugar, eggs and vanilla in large bowl until well blended. Stir together flour, cocoa, baking soda and salt; add alternately with water to shortening mixture. Stir in oats, 1 cup chocolate chips, 1 cup coconut and nuts, blending well. Cover; refrigerate 2 hours.

2. Heat oven to 350°F. Lightly grease cookie sheet or line with parchment paper. Using ¹/₄-cup ice cream scoop or measuring cup, drop dough about 4 inches apart onto prepared cookie sheet. Sprinkle cookie tops with remaining coconut. Top with remaining chocolate chips (about 9 chips per cookie); lightly press into dough.

3. Bake 10 to 12 minutes or until set (do not overbake). Cool slightly; remove from cookie sheet to wire rack. Cool completely.

✳ *Makes about 4 dozen cookies*

Double Striped Peanut Butter Oatmeal Cookies

³/₄ cup REESE'S® Creamy Peanut Butter
¹/₂ cup (1 stick) butter or margarine, softened
¹/₃ cup granulated sugar
¹/₃ cup packed light brown sugar
1 egg
2 tablespoons milk
1 teaspoon vanilla extract
1¹/₃ cups uncooked quick-cooking oats, divided
1 cup all-purpose flour
1 teaspoon baking soda
¹/₂ teaspoon salt
¹/₂ cup HERSHEY'S Milk Chocolate Chips
2 teaspoons shortening (do not use butter, margarine, spread or oil)
¹/₂ cup REESE'S® Peanut Butter Chips

1. Heat oven to 350°F. Beat peanut butter and butter in large bowl until well blended. Add granulated sugar and brown sugar; beat until fluffy. Add egg, milk and vanilla; beat well. Stir together ¹/₂ cup oats, flour, baking soda and salt; gradually beat into peanut butter mixture.

2. Shape dough into 1-inch balls. Roll in remaining oats; place on ungreased cookie sheet. Flatten cookies with tines of fork to form a crisscross pattern.

3. Bake 10 to 12 minutes or until lightly browned. Cool slightly; remove from cookie sheet to wire rack. Cool completely.

4. Place chocolate chips and 1 teaspoon shortening in medium microwave-safe container. Microwave at medium (50%) 30 seconds; stir. If necessary, microwave at medium an additional 10 seconds at a time, stirring after each heating, until chocolate is melted and smooth when stirred. Drizzle over cookies. Repeat procedure with peanut butter chips and remaining 1 teaspoon shortening. Allow drizzles to set.

Breakfast-Time Favorites

※ *Makes 4 servings*

Tropical Fruit Breakfast Parfaits

- 4 containers (6 ounces each) vanilla yogurt
- 1 medium banana, mashed
- 2 tablespoons maple syrup
- ³/₄ to 1 teaspoon ground cinnamon
- 1 cup honey-sweetened oat flakes cereal
- ¹/₂ cup sweetened flaked coconut
- 1 can (8 ounces) crushed pineapple in juice, drained
- 2 cups strawberries, quartered
- 1 medium kiwi, peeled and diced

Stir yogurt, banana, syrup and cinnamon in medium bowl until well blended. Spoon about ¹/₃ cup into 4 parfait or wine glasses. Top each with equal parts oat flakes, coconut and fruit.

Variations: Substitute plain yogurt for vanilla yogurt. Substitute honey for maple syrup.

> Oats of Wisdom: Prepare yogurt mixture the night before. Cover and refrigerate until serving time.

Sunny Seed Bran Waffles

  2 egg whites
  1 tablespoon dark brown sugar
  1 tablespoon canola or vegetable oil
  1 cup milk
  $^2/_3$ cup unprocessed wheat bran
  $^2/_3$ cup uncooked quick oats
1$^1/_2$ teaspoons baking powder
  $^1/_4$ teaspoon salt
  3 tablespoons toasted sunflower seeds*
  1 cup apple butter

To toast sunflower seeds, cook and stir in small nonstick skillet over medium heat about 5 minutes or until golden brown. Remove from skillet.

1. Beat egg whites in medium bowl with electric mixer until soft peaks form; set aside. Mix sugar and oil in small bowl. Stir in milk; mix well. Combine bran, oats, baking powder and salt in large bowl; mix well. Stir sugar mixture into bran mixture. Add sunflower seeds; stir just until moistened. *Do not overmix.* Gently fold in beaten egg whites.

2. Spray nonstick waffle iron lightly with nonstick cooking spray; heat according to manufacturer's directions. Spoon $^1/_2$ cup batter onto waffle iron for each waffle. Cook until steam stops escaping from around edges and waffle is golden brown. Serve each waffle with $^1/_4$ cup apple butter.

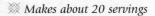

Fruited Granola

3 cups uncooked quick oats
1 cup sliced almonds
1 cup honey
1/2 cup wheat germ or honey wheat germ
3 tablespoons butter or margarine, melted
1 teaspoon ground cinnamon
3 cups whole grain cereal flakes
1/2 cup dried blueberries
1/2 cup dried cranberries
1/2 cup dried banana chips

1. Preheat oven to 325°F.

2. Spread oats and almonds in single layer in 13×9-inch baking pan. Bake 10 to 15 minutes or until lightly toasted, stirring frequently.

3. Combine honey, wheat germ, butter and cinnamon in large bowl until well blended. Add oats and almonds; toss to coat completely. Spread mixture in single layer in baking pan. Bake 20 minutes or until golden brown. Cool completely in pan on wire rack. Break mixture into chunks.

4. Combine oat chunks, cereal, blueberries, cranberries and banana chips in large bowl. Store in airtight container at room temperature up to 2 weeks.

> Oats of Wisdom: Prepare this granola on the weekend and you'll have a scrumptious snack or breakfast treat on hand for the rest of the week!

Banana Bread Oatmeal

3 cups fat-free (skim) milk
3 tablespoons packed brown sugar
³/₄ teaspoon ground cinnamon
¹/₄ teaspoon ground nutmeg
¹/₄ teaspoon salt (optional)
2 cups QUAKER® Oats (quick or old fashioned, uncooked)
2 medium-size ripe bananas, mashed (about 1 cup)
2 to 3 tablespoons coarsely chopped toasted pecans
Vanilla fat-free yogurt (optional)
Banana slices (optional)
Pecan halves (optional)

1. Bring milk, brown sugar, spices and salt, if desired, to a gentle boil in medium saucepan (watch carefully). Stir in oats. Return to a boil; reduce heat to medium. Cook 1 minute for quick oats, 5 minutes for old fashioned oats, or until most of liquid is absorbed, stirring occasionally.

2. Remove oatmeal from heat. Stir in mashed bananas and pecans. Spoon oatmeal into 4 cereal bowls. Top with yogurt, sliced bananas and pecan halves, if desired.

Cook's Tip: To toast nuts, spread in single layer on cookie sheet. Bake at 350°F about 6 to 8 minutes or until lightly browned and fragrant, stirring occasionally. Cool before using. Or spread in single layer on microwave-safe plate. Microwave on HIGH (100% power) 1 minute; stir. Continue to microwave on HIGH, checking every 30 seconds, until nuts are fragrant and brown. Cool before using.

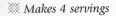

Baked Oatmeal with Apricots

　1 cup uncooked old-fashioned oats
　1 teaspoon ground cinnamon, divided
　¼ teaspoon salt
1½ cups milk
　1 egg
　2 tablespoons honey
　2 teaspoons butter, melted
　1 teaspoon vanilla
　1 cup chopped peeled apple
　3 tablespoons finely chopped dried apricots
　¼ cup chopped nuts (optional)

1. Preheat oven to 350°F. Lightly coat 1½- to 2-quart baking dish with nonstick cooking spray.

2. Combine oats, ½ teaspoon cinnamon and salt in medium bowl. Combine milk, egg, honey, butter and vanilla in separate medium bowl; stir into oat mixture. Stir in apple and apricots.

3. Pour mixture into prepared baking dish. Sprinkle with remaining ½ teaspoon cinnamon. Bake 40 to 45 minutes or until knife inserted into center comes out clean. Let stand 5 minutes before serving. Sprinkle nuts over top, if desired.

Prep Time: 10 minutes ❋ **Cook Time:** 40 to 45 minutes

Oatmeal Pecan Pancakes

1¼ to 1½ cups milk, divided
½ cup uncooked old-fashioned oats
⅔ cup all-purpose flour
⅓ cup whole wheat flour
2½ tablespoons packed light brown sugar
2 teaspoons baking powder
½ teaspoon baking soda
¼ teaspoon salt
1 egg
2 tablespoons melted butter
½ cup chopped toasted pecans
Maple syrup (optional)

1. Bring ½ cup milk to a simmer in small saucepan. Stir in oats. Remove from heat; set aside 10 minutes.

2. Combine flours, brown sugar, baking powder, baking soda and salt in large bowl; mix well.

3. Combine egg and melted butter in small bowl; mix well. Stir in oatmeal mixture and ¾ cup milk. Add egg mixture to dry ingredients; stir just to combine. If mixture is too thick to spoon, add remaining ¼ cup milk, 1 tablespoon at a time. Add pecans; stir just to combine.

4. Lightly butter large skillet or griddle; heat over medium heat. Working in batches, drop batter by ¼ cupfuls. Cook about 2 minutes until tops are bubbly and bottoms are golden brown. Flip; cook until golden brown. Repeat with remaining pancake batter. Serve immediately.

Oatmeal Crème Brûlée

4 cups water
3 cups uncooked quick-cooking oats
$1/2$ teaspoon salt
6 egg yolks
$1/2$ cup granulated sugar
2 cups whipping cream
1 teaspoon vanilla
$1/4$ cup packed light brown sugar
Fresh berries (optional)

SLOW COOKER DIRECTIONS

1. Coat slow cooker with nonstick cooking spray. Cover and set on HIGH to heat. Meanwhile, bring water to a boil. Immediately pour into preheated slow cooker. Stir in oats and salt. Cover.

2. Combine egg yolks and granulated sugar in small bowl. Mix well; set aside. Heat cream and vanilla in medium saucepan over medium heat until mixture begins to simmer. *Do not boil.* Remove from heat. Whisk $1/2$ cup hot cream into yolks, stirring rapidly so yolks don't cook.* Whisk warmed egg mixture into cream, stirring rapidly to blend well. Spoon mixture over oatmeal. Do not stir.

3. Turn slow cooker to LOW. Line lid with 2 paper towels. Cover; cook on LOW 3 to $3^{1}/2$ hours or until custard is set.

4. Uncover and sprinkle brown sugar over surface of custard. Line lid with 2 dry paper towels. Cover; continue cooking on LOW 10 to 15 minutes or until brown sugar has melted. Serve with fresh berries, if desired.

Place bowl on damp towel to prevent slipping.

Prep Time: 15 minutes ※ **Cook Time:** 3 to $3^{1}/2$ hours

Caramel-Nut Sticky Biscuits

TOPPING

- 2/3 cup firmly packed brown sugar
- 1/4 cup light corn syrup
- 1/4 cup (1/2 stick) margarine, melted
- 1/2 teaspoon ground cinnamon
- 1 cup pecan halves

BISCUITS

- 2 cups all-purpose flour
- 1 cup QUAKER® Oats (quick or old fashioned, uncooked)
- 1/4 cup granulated sugar
- 1 tablespoon baking powder
- 3/4 teaspoon baking soda
- 1/2 teaspoon salt (optional)
- 1/2 teaspoon ground cinnamon
- 1/3 cup (5 1/3 tablespoons) margarine
- 1 cup buttermilk*

Sour milk can be substituted for buttermilk. For 1 cup sour milk, combine 1 tablespoon vinegar or lemon juice and enough milk to make 1 cup; let stand 5 minutes.

Heat oven to 425°F. For topping, combine first four ingredients; mix well. Spread onto bottom of 9-inch square baking pan. Sprinkle with pecans; set aside. For biscuits, combine dry ingredients; mix well. Cut in margarine with pastry blender or two knives until crumbly. Stir in buttermilk, mixing just until moistened. Knead gently on lightly floured surface 5 to 7 times; pat into 8-inch square. Cut with knife into sixteen 2-inch square biscuits; place over topping in pan. Bake 25 to 28 minutes or until golden brown. Let stand 3 minutes; invert onto large platter. Serve warm.

Fabulous Fruit Desserts

Strawberry and Peach Crisp

1 cup frozen unsweetened peach slices, thawed and cut into
    1-inch pieces
1 cup sliced fresh strawberries
3 teaspoons sugar, divided
$\frac{1}{4}$ cup bran cereal flakes
2 tablespoons uncooked old-fashioned oats
1 tablespoon all-purpose flour
$\frac{1}{8}$ teaspoon ground cinnamon
$\frac{1}{8}$ teaspoon salt
1 tablespoon unsalted butter, cut into small pieces

1. Preheat oven to 325°F. Coat 1- to 1$\frac{1}{2}$-quart glass baking dish with
nonstick cooking spray. Set aside.

2. Combine peaches, strawberries and 1 teaspoon sugar in medium
bowl. Transfer to prepared baking dish.

3. Combine cereal, oats, flour, remaining 2 teaspoons sugar, cinnamon
and salt in small bowl. Add butter; stir with fork until mixture resembles
coarse crumbs. Sprinkle over fruit. Bake 20 minutes or until fruit is
heated through and topping is slightly browned.

Variation: If you like the flavor of brown sugar, you may substitute
2 teaspoons of packed brown sugar for the 2 teaspoons of granulated
sugar in the topping.

Variation: To make a strawberry crisp, omit the peaches and use 2 cups
strawberries in the recipe.

Apple Cinnamon Rice Crisp

1 cup MINUTE® White or Brown Rice, uncooked
 Nonstick cooking spray
1 can (20 ounces) apple pie filling
1 cup packed brown sugar, divided
½ cup raisins
½ cup walnuts, chopped
1 teaspoon ground cinnamon
1½ cups uncooked rolled oats
4 tablespoons margarine
 Vanilla ice cream (optional)

Prepare rice according to package directions. Preheat oven to 350°F.
Spray 2-quart baking dish with nonstick cooking spray. Combine
rice, pie filling, ½ cup brown sugar, raisins, walnuts and cinnamon
in medium bowl. Pour into prepared dish. In same bowl, combine
remaining ½ cup brown sugar and rolled oats. Cut in margarine with
pastry blender or fork, mixing well until mixture is moist. Sprinkle over
rice mixture. Bake 20 minutes. Serve with ice cream, if desired.

※ *Makes 6 to 8 servings*

Apple Crumble Pot

FILLING

²/₃ cup packed dark brown sugar
2 tablespoons biscuit baking mix
1¹/₂ teaspoons ground cinnamon
¹/₄ teaspoon ground allspice
4 Granny Smith apples (about 2 pounds), cored and cut into 8 wedges each
¹/₂ cup dried cranberries
2 tablespoons butter, cubed
1 teaspoon vanilla

TOPPING

1 cup biscuit baking mix
¹/₂ cup uncooked old-fashioned oats
¹/₃ cup packed dark brown sugar
3 tablespoons cold butter, cubed
¹/₂ cup chopped pecans

SLOW COOKER DIRECTIONS

1. Coat slow cooker with nonstick cooking spray. Combine ²/₃ cup brown sugar, 2 tablespoons baking mix, cinnamon and allspice in large bowl. Add remaining filling ingredients; toss to coat. Transfer to slow cooker.

2. Combine 1 cup baking mix, oats and ¹/₂ cup brown sugar in large bowl. Cut in butter with pastry blender or 2 knives until mixture resembles pea-sized crumbs. Sprinkle evenly over filling; top with pecans. Cover; cook on HIGH 2¹/₄ hours or until apples are tender. *Do not overcook.*

3. Turn off slow cooker. Uncover and let stand 15 to 30 minutes before serving. Garnish as desired.

Prep Time: 15 minutes ※ **Cook Time:** 2¹/₄ hours

Cranberry Peach Almond Dessert

2 bags (16 ounces each) frozen unsweetened peach slices
1 cup dried sweetened cranberries
1 teaspoon vanilla
1/2 teaspoon almond extract (optional)
1/2 cup uncooked old-fashioned oats
1/3 cup packed dark brown sugar
1/4 cup all-purpose flour
1/2 teaspoon ground cinnamon
1/4 cup (1/2 stick) cold butter
1/4 cup slivered almonds

1. Preheat oven to 350°F. Thaw peaches; do not drain. Transfer fruit to 9-inch deep dish pie pan or baking pan. Stir in cranberries, vanilla and almond extract, if desired.

2. Combine oats, brown sugar, flour and cinnamon in medium bowl. Cut in butter with pastry blender or 2 knives until mixture resembles coarse crumbs. Stir in almonds; sprinkle mixture evenly over peaches.

3. Bake 40 minutes or until peaches are tender and topping is golden brown.

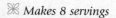

Oats 'n' Apple Tart

1½ cups uncooked quick oats
½ cup packed brown sugar, divided
1 tablespoon plus ¼ teaspoon ground cinnamon, divided
5 tablespoons butter or margarine, melted
2 medium Golden Delicious apples, cored and thinly sliced
1 teaspoon lemon juice
¼ cup water
1 envelope unflavored gelatin
½ cup apple juice concentrate
1 package (8 ounces) cream cheese, softened
⅛ teaspoon ground nutmeg

1. Preheat oven to 350°F. Combine oats, ¼ cup brown sugar and 1 tablespoon cinnamon in medium bowl. Add butter and stir until combined. Press onto bottom and up side of 9-inch pie plate. Bake 7 minutes or until set. Cool on wire rack.

2. Toss apple slices with lemon juice in small bowl; set aside. Place water in small saucepan. Sprinkle gelatin over water; let stand 3 to 5 minutes. Add apple juice concentrate; cook and stir over medium heat until gelatin is dissolved. *Do not boil.* Remove from heat; set aside.

3. Beat cream cheese in medium bowl with electric mixer at medium speed until fluffy and smooth. Add remaining ¼ cup brown sugar, ¼ teaspoon cinnamon and nutmeg. Mix until smooth. Slowly beat in gelatin mixture on low speed until blended and creamy, about 1 minute. *Do not overbeat.*

4. Arrange apple slices in crust. Spread cream cheese mixture evenly over top. Refrigerate 2 hours or until set.

※ *Makes 10 to 12 servings*

Apple Toffee Crisp

   5 cups (about 5 medium apples) peeled and sliced Granny Smith
      apples
   5 cups (about 5 medium apples) peeled and sliced McIntosh
      apples
1¼ cups sugar, divided
1¼ cups all-purpose flour, divided
 ¾ cup (1½ sticks) butter or margarine, divided
1⅓ cups (8-ounce package) HEATH® BITS 'O BRICKLE® Toffee Bits
   1 cup uncooked rolled oats
 ½ teaspoon ground cinnamon
 ¼ teaspoon baking powder
 ¼ teaspoon baking soda
 ¼ teaspoon salt
   Whipped topping or ice cream (optional)

1. Heat oven to 375°F. Grease 13×9×2-inch baking pan.

2. Toss apple slices, ¾ cup sugar and ¼ cup flour in large bowl, coating
apples evenly. Spread in bottom of prepared pan. Dot with ¼ cup
(½ stick) butter.

3. Stir together toffee bits, oats, remaining ½ cup sugar, remaining
1 cup flour, cinnamon, baking powder, baking soda and salt. Melt
remaining ½ cup (1 stick) butter; add to oat mixture, mixing until
crumbs are formed. Sprinkle crumb mixture over apples.

4. Bake 45 to 50 minutes or until topping is lightly browned and apples
are tender. Serve warm with whipped topping or ice cream, if desired.
Cover; refrigerate leftovers.

Rustic Plum Tart

¼ cup (½ stick) plus 1 tablespoon butter, divided
3 cups plum wedges (about 6 plums, see Tip)
¼ cup granulated sugar
½ cup all-purpose flour
½ cup uncooked old-fashioned oats
¼ cup packed brown sugar
½ teaspoon ground cinnamon
¼ teaspoon salt
1 egg
1 teaspoon water
1 refrigerated pie crust (half of 15-ounce package)
1 tablespoon chopped crystallized ginger

1. Preheat oven to 425°F. Line baking sheet with parchment paper.

2. Melt 1 tablespoon butter in large skillet over high heat. Add plums; cook and stir about 3 minutes or until plums begin to break down. Stir in granulated sugar; cook 1 minute or until juices have thickened. Remove from heat; set aside.

3. Combine flour, oats, brown sugar, cinnamon and salt in medium bowl. Cut in remaining ¼ cup butter with pastry blender or 2 knives until mixture resembles coarse crumbs.

4. Beat egg and water in small bowl. Unroll pie crust on prepared baking sheet. Brush crust lightly with egg mixture. Sprinkle with ¼ cup oat mixture, leaving 2-inch border around edge of crust. Spoon plums over oat mixture, leaving juices in skillet. Sprinkle with ginger. Fold crust up around plums, overlapping as necessary. Sprinkle with remaining oat mixture. Brush edge of crust with egg mixture.

5. Bake 25 minutes or until golden brown. Cool slightly before serving.

Oats of Wisdom: For this recipe, use dark reddish-purple plums and cut the fruit into 8 wedges.

❀ *Makes 8 servings*

Double Cherry Crumbles

1/2 (about 18-ounce) package refrigerated oatmeal raisin cookie
dough*
1/2 cup uncooked old-fashioned oats
3/4 teaspoon ground cinnamon
1/2 teaspoon ground ginger
2 tablespoons cold butter, cut into small pieces
1 cup chopped pecans, toasted**
1 bag (16 ounces) frozen pitted unsweetened dark sweet cherries,
thawed
2 cans (21 ounces each) cherry pie filling

Save remaining 1/2 package of dough for another use.

**To toast pecans, spread in single layer on baking sheet. Bake in preheated 350°F
oven 7 to 10 minutes or until golden brown, stirring frequently.*

1. Let dough stand at room temperature about 15 minutes. Preheat
oven to 350°F. Lightly grease 8 (1/2-cup) ramekins; place on baking
sheet.

2. For topping, beat dough, oats, cinnamon and ginger in large bowl
with electric mixer at medium speed until well blended. Cut in butter
with pastry blender or 2 knives until large crumbs form. Stir in pecans.

3. Combine cherries and pie filling in large bowl. Divide cherry mixture
evenly among prepared ramekins; sprinkle with topping. Bake about
25 minutes or until topping is browned. Serve warm.

Bar Cookie Bonanza

Oatmeal Date Bars

2 packages (about 18 ounces each) refrigerated oatmeal raisin
   cookie dough
2½ cups uncooked old-fashioned oats, divided
2 packages (8 ounces each) chopped dates
1 cup water
½ cup sugar
1 teaspoon vanilla

1. Let doughs stand at room temperature about 15 minutes. Preheat oven to 350°F. Lightly grease 13×9-inch baking pan.

2. Combine three fourths of one package of dough and 1 cup oats in medium bowl; beat until well blended. Set aside.

3. Combine remaining 1¼ packages dough and remaining 1½ cups oats in large bowl; beat until well blended. Press dough evenly onto bottom of prepared pan. Bake 10 minutes.

4. Meanwhile, combine dates, water and sugar in medium saucepan; bring to a boil over high heat. Boil 3 minutes; remove from heat and stir in vanilla. Spread date mixture evenly over partially baked crust; sprinkle evenly with topping mixture.

5. Bake 25 to 28 minutes or until bubbly. Cool completely in pan on wire rack.

※ ※ ※

✳ *Makes 3 dozen bars*

Pear Hazelnut Bars

  1 recipe Basic Short Dough (page 66)
  4 cups chopped, peeled, fresh pears
  1/2 cup raisins
  2 tablespoons fresh lemon juice
  2 tablespoons all-purpose flour
  2 tablespoons granulated sugar
  1 teaspoon grated lemon peel
  1/2 teaspoon ground cinnamon

CRUMB TOPPING
  1/2 cup all-purpose flour
  1/2 cup packed brown sugar
  1/2 teaspoon ground cinnamon
  1/2 cup (1 stick) cold butter, cubed
  1/2 cup uncooked old-fashioned oats
  1/2 cup chopped hazelnuts

1. Preheat oven to 350°F. Line 13×9-inch baking pan with foil, leaving 1-inch overhang. Spray foil with nonstick cooking spray.

2. Prepare Basic Short Dough. Press dough evenly into pan. Bake 25 minutes or until lightly browned. Set aside on wire rack.

3. Meanwhile, mix pears, raisins, lemon juice, 2 tablespoons flour, granulated sugar, lemon peel and 1/2 teaspoon cinnamon in large bowl. Spread over warm crust.

4. Combine 1/2 cup flour, brown sugar and remaining 1/2 teaspoon cinnamon in medium bowl. Cut in butter with pastry blender or 2 knives until mixture resembles coarse crumbs. Stir in oats and hazelnuts. Sprinkle topping evenly over filling, lightly pressing into place.

5. Bake 30 minutes or until topping is golden brown. Cool completely in pan on wire rack.

6. Refrigerate bars at least 2 hours before serving. Remove foil from bars; cut into squares. Cut each square diagonally into triangles. Store covered in refrigerator.

✳ ✳ ✳

Chocolate 'n' Oat Bars

1 cup all-purpose flour
1 cup uncooked quick-cooking oats
¾ cup firmly packed light brown sugar
½ cup (1 stick) butter or margarine, softened
1 (14-ounce) can EAGLE BRAND® Sweetened Condensed Milk
    (NOT evaporated milk)
1 cup chopped nuts
1 cup (6 ounces) semisweet chocolate chips

1. Preheat oven to 350°F (325°F for glass dish). In large bowl, combine flour, oats, brown sugar and butter; mix well. (Mixture will be crumbly.) Reserve ½ cup oat mixture and press remainder on bottom of 13×9-inch baking pan. Bake 10 minutes.

2. Pour EAGLE BRAND® evenly over crust. Sprinkle with nuts and chocolate chips. Top with reserved oat mixture; press down firmly.

3. Bake 25 minutes or until lightly browned. Cool. Chill if desired. Cut into bars. Store leftovers covered at room temperature.

Prep Time: 15 minutes ✳ **Bake Time:** 35 minutes

✳ *Makes about 2 dozen bars*

Ooey-Gooey Caramel Peanut Butter Bars

1 package (about 18 ounces) yellow cake mix without pudding in
    the mix
1 cup uncooked old-fashioned oats
²/₃ cup creamy peanut butter
1 egg, slightly beaten
2 tablespoons milk
1 package (8 ounces) cream cheese, softened
1 jar (about 12 ounces) caramel ice cream topping
1 cup semisweet chocolate chips

1. Preheat oven to 350°F. Lightly grease 13×9-inch baking pan.

2. Combine cake mix and oats in large bowl. Cut in peanut butter with pastry blender or 2 knives until mixture is crumbly.

3. Blend egg and milk in small bowl. Add to peanut butter mixture; stir just until combined. Reserve 1½ cups mixture. Press remaining peanut butter mixture into prepared pan.

4. Beat cream cheese in medium bowl with electric mixer at medium speed until fluffy. Add caramel topping; beat just until combined. Carefully spread over peanut butter layer in pan. Crumble reserved peanut butter mixture into small pieces; sprinkle over cream cheese layer. Sprinkle with chocolate chips.

5. Bake 30 minutes or until nearly set in center. Cool completely in pan on wire rack.

Candy Bar Bars

¾ cup (1½ sticks) butter or margarine, softened
¼ cup peanut butter
1 cup firmly packed light brown sugar
1 teaspoon baking soda
2 cups uncooked quick-cooking oats
1½ cups all-purpose flour
1 egg
1 (14-ounce) can EAGLE BRAND® Sweetened Condensed Milk
  (NOT evaporated milk)
4 cups chopped candy bars (such as chocolate-covered caramel-
  topped nougat bars with peanuts, chocolate-covered crisp
  wafers, chocolate-covered caramel-topped cookie bars or
  chocolate-covered peanut butter cups)

1. Preheat oven to 350°F. In large bowl, combine butter and peanut butter until smooth; add brown sugar and baking soda. Beat well; stir in oats and flour. Reserve 1¾ cups crumb mixture.

2. Stir egg into remaining crumb mixture in bowl. Press crumb mixture firmly on bottom of ungreased 15×10-inch baking pan. Bake 15 minutes. Remove from oven.

3. Spread EAGLE BRAND® over hot crust. Stir together reserved crumb mixture and candy bar pieces; sprinkle evenly over top.

4. Bake 25 minutes or until golden brown. Cool. Cut into bars. Store leftovers loosely covered at room temperature.

Prep Time: 15 minutes ✳ **Bake Time:** 40 minutes

Hikers' Bar Cookies

³/₄ cup all-purpose flour
¹/₂ cup packed brown sugar
¹/₂ cup uncooked quick oats
¹/₄ cup toasted wheat germ
¹/₄ cup unsweetened applesauce
¹/₄ cup (¹/₂ stick) butter, softened
¹/₈ teaspoon salt
 2 eggs
¹/₄ cup raisins
¹/₄ cup dried cranberries
¹/₄ cup sunflower kernels
 1 tablespoon grated orange peel
 1 teaspoon ground cinnamon

1. Preheat oven to 350°F. Lightly coat 13×9-inch baking pan with nonstick cooking spray; set aside.

2. Beat flour, sugar, oats, wheat germ, applesauce, butter and salt in large bowl with electric mixer at medium speed until well blended. Stir in eggs, raisins, cranberries, sunflower kernels, orange peel and cinnamon. Spread into pan.

3. Bake 15 minutes or until firm. Cool completely in pan on wire rack. Cut into 24 squares.

✳ *Makes about 24 bars*

Whole Grain Cereal Bars

5 to 6 cups assorted whole grain cereals
1 package (10 ounces) large marshmallows
¹/₄ cup (¹/₂ stick) butter
¹/₄ cup uncooked old-fashioned oats

1. Crush large chunks of cereal by placing in resealable food storage bag and lightly rolling over bag with rolling pin. Grease 13×9-inch baking pan.

2. Heat marshmallows and butter in large saucepan over medium-low heat, stirring until melted and smooth. Remove pan from heat.

3. Stir in cereal until well blended. Using buttered hands or waxed paper to prevent sticking, pat cereal mixture evenly into prepared pan. Sprinkle with oats. Cool at room temperature until firm. Cut into bars.

✳ *Makes enough dough for 36 bar cookies*

Basic Short Dough

³/₄ cup sugar
³/₄ cup (1¹/₂ sticks) butter
1 tablespoon grated lemon peel
3 egg yolks
1 teaspoon vanilla
2 cups all-purpose flour
¹/₄ teaspoon salt

Beat sugar, butter and lemon peel in large bowl with electric mixer at medium speed 1 minute. Beat in egg yolks and vanilla until well blended. Scrape down bowl. Add flour and salt; mix just until combined.

✳ *Makes 24 bars*

O'Henrietta Bars

MAZOLA PURE® Cooking Spray
1/2 cup (1 stick) butter or margarine, softened
1/2 cup packed brown sugar
1/2 cup KARO® Light or Dark Corn Syrup
1 teaspoon vanilla
3 cups quick oats, uncooked
1/2 cup (3 ounces) semi-sweet chocolate chips
1/4 cup creamy peanut butter

1. Preheat oven to 350°F. Spray 8- or 9-inch square baking pan with cooking spray.

2. Beat butter, brown sugar, corn syrup and vanilla in large bowl with mixer at medium speed until smooth. Stir in oats. Press into prepared pan.

3. Bake 25 minutes or until center is barely firm. Cool on wire rack 5 minutes.

4. Sprinkle with chocolate chips; top with small spoonfuls of peanut butter. Let stand 5 minutes; spread peanut butter and chocolate over bars, swirling to marble.

5. Cool completely on wire rack before cutting. Cut into bars; refrigerate 15 minutes to set topping.

Prep Time: 20 minutes ✳ **Bake Time:** 25 minutes, plus cooling

Main Dish Magic

Turkey Meat Loaf

1 pound ground turkey
¾ cup uncooked quick oats
1 cup tomato sauce, divided
1 small onion, finely chopped
1 egg
1 teaspoon salt

1. Preheat oven to 350°F. Spray 9×5-inch loaf pan with nonstick cooking spray.

2. Combine turkey, oats, ½ cup tomato sauce, onion, egg and salt in large bowl; mix well. Shape into loaf; place in prepared pan.

3. Bake 45 minutes to 1 hour or until browned and cooked through (165°F). Top with remaining sauce; bake 5 minutes. Remove from pan; cut into slices.

Note: Ketchup or salsa can be substituted for the tomato sauce.

> Oats of Wisdom: After removing the baked meat loaf from the oven, run knife around the edges, then let it stand for 10 minutes. This allows the meat loaf to set and will make slicing easier.

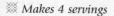

 Makes 4 servings

Chicken and Veggie Meatballs with Fennel

1 pound ground chicken
½ cup finely chopped green onion
½ cup finely chopped green bell pepper
⅓ cup oatmeal
¼ cup grated Parmesan cheese
¼ cup shredded carrots
2 egg whites
2 garlic cloves, minced
½ teaspoon dried Italian seasoning
¼ teaspoon salt
¼ teaspoon dried fennel seed
⅛ teaspoon red pepper flakes (optional)
1 teaspoon extra-virgin olive oil
  Pasta sauce

1. Combine all ingredients except oil and pasta sauce in large mixing bowl. Shape into 36 balls, each about 1 inch in diameter.

2. Heat oil in large nonstick skillet over medium-high heat. Add meatballs; cook 10 minutes or until no longer pink in center, turning frequently. Use fork and spoon for easy turning. Serve immediately with pasta sauce.

Note: To freeze meatballs, cool completely and place in large freezer resealable food storage bag. Release any excess air from bag and seal. Freeze bag flat for easier storage and faster thawing. To thaw, remove amount of meatballs needed from freezer bag and reseal bag, releasing any excess air. Place meatballs on a microwavable plate and cook on HIGH 20 to 30 seconds.

Old-Fashioned Meat Loaf

1 teaspoon olive oil
1 cup finely chopped onion
4 cloves garlic, minced
1½ pounds ground beef
1 cup chili sauce, divided
¾ cup uncooked old-fashioned oats
2 egg whites
½ teaspoon black pepper
¼ teaspoon salt
1 tablespoon Dijon mustard

1. Preheat oven to 375°F. Heat oil in large nonstick skillet over medium heat. Add onion; cook and stir 5 minutes. Add garlic; cook 1 minute. Remove from heat; transfer to large bowl. Let cool 5 minutes.

2. Add beef, ½ cup chili sauce, oats, egg whites, pepper and salt; mix well. Pack into 9×5-inch loaf pan. Combine remaining ½ cup chili sauce and mustard in small bowl; spoon evenly over top of meat loaf.

3. Bake 45 to 50 minutes or until cooked through (160°F). Let stand 5 minutes. Pour off any juices from pan. Cut into slices to serve.

Nancy's Grilled Turkey Meatballs

1 pound lean ground turkey breast
$^{1}/_{2}$ cup uncooked old-fashioned oats
$^{1}/_{4}$ cup fresh whole wheat bread crumbs
1 egg white
3 tablespoons Parmesan cheese
2 tablespoons *French's*® Honey Dijon Mustard
$^{1}/_{4}$ teaspoon crushed garlic
$^{1}/_{4}$ teaspoon ground black pepper
1 cup pineapple chunks or wedges
1 small red bell pepper, cut into squares

1. Combine turkey, oats, bread crumbs, egg white, cheese, mustard, garlic and black pepper in large bowl. Mix well and form into 24 meatballs.

2. Place 4 meatballs on each skewer, alternating with pineapple and bell pepper.

3. Cook meatballs 10 minutes on well-greased grill over medium heat until no longer pink inside, turning often. Serve with additional *French's*® Honey Dijon Mustard on the side for dipping.

Prep Time: 15 minutes ※ **Cook Time:** 10 minutes

Oats of Wisdom: Combine $^{1}/_{3}$ cup each *French's*®
Honey Dijon Mustard, honey and *Frank's*® *RedHot*®
Cayenne Pepper Sauce. Use for dipping grilled wings,
ribs and chicken.

Spicy Oat-Crusted Chicken with Sunshine Salsa

SUNSHINE SALSA

$^3/_4$ **cup prepared salsa**

$^3/_4$ **cup coarsely chopped orange sections**

CHICKEN

2 **tablespoons canola oil**

1 **tablespoon margarine, melted**

2 **teaspoons chili powder**

1 **teaspoon garlic powder**

1 **teaspoon ground cumin**

$^3/_4$ **teaspoon salt**

1$^1/_2$ **cups Quick QUAKER® Oats, uncooked**

1 **egg, lightly beaten**

1 **tablespoon water**

4 **boneless, skinless chicken breast halves**
(about 5 to 6 ounces each)

Chopped fresh cilantro (optional)

1. Combine salsa and orange sections in small bowl. Refrigerate, covered, until serving time.

2. Heat oven to 375°F. Line baking sheet with aluminum foil. Stir together oil, margarine, chili powder, garlic powder, cumin and salt in flat, shallow dish. Add oats, stirring until evenly moistened.

3. Beat egg and water with fork until frothy in second flat, shallow dish. Dip chicken into egg mixture, then coat completely in seasoned oats. Place chicken on foil-lined baking sheet. Pat any extra oat mixture onto top of chicken.

4. Bake 30 minutes or until chicken is cooked through and oat coating is golden brown. Serve with salsa. Garnish with cilantro, if desired.

Acknowledgments

The publisher would like to thank the companies listed below for the use of their recipes in this publication.

ACH Food Companies, Inc.

Dole Food Company, Inc.

EAGLE BRAND®

The Hershey Company

©Mars, Incorporated 2009

Minnesota Cultivated Wild Rice Council

Nestlé USA

The Quaker® Oatmeal Kitchens

Reckitt Benckiser Inc.

Riviana Foods Inc.